The Official Rules
at
HOME

The Official Rules
— at —
HOME

*The Laws That Determine What Can, and
Probably Will, Go Awry in
Your Daily Life*

Paul Dickson

BARNES
&NOBLE
BOOKS
NEW YORK

Published by Galahad Books
A division of BBS Publishing Corporation
450 Raritan Center Parkway
Edison, NJ 08837

By arrangement with Walker & Company.

This edition distributed by Barnes & Noble Books.

Library of Congress Control Number: 96-12171

ISBN: 0-7607-5457-8

Printed in the United States of America.

The Official Rules
at
HOME

CALAMITAS NECESSARIA EST

Introduction

The Murphy Center for the Codification of Human and Organizational Law was founded in 1976 by the author of this book, who was its first Director, and, has been, since 1989, its self-appointed Director for Life. Mainly inspired by Murphy's Law ("If anything can go wrong it will"), the Center has pioneered research into some of the major givens of the twentieth century: that a wrong number will displace a body immersed in water, that a defective pay phone will find your last quarter, and that you, personally, will be sought out by the only shopping cart with a defective wheel. It proved that if you only watch one episode of a television show during the regular season and turn on that show during the rerun season, you will always see the same episode.

Now in its twentieth year, the Center is beginning a series of books that will help people in separate realms of their lives. This book takes on home and family life, and its companion volume, *The Official Rules at Work*, covers life on the job. Other collections are planned on lawyers and politicians; life, love, and the pursuit of happiness; computers and technology; travel and transportation; and a half-dozen other topics. These collections draw on the more than 7,000 laws that have been sent to the Center over the past twenty years. Some have appeared in previous general collections; many appear here in book form for the first time.

Lest there be any question, these laws, rules, observations, and maxims are meant to make life easier. I have one taped to the visor of my car that simply reminds me "You're Not Late Until You Get There." Another helpful maxim that comes into play when, say, you are late because of a flat tire is *Burnham's Tenth Law:* If there's no alternative, there's no problem.

There is no household contingency for which I do not have a rule to help me cope. Whenever I work around the house, for example, I always take comfort in *The Poorman Flaw:* In any home-improvement project, there will be one mistake so gross that the only solution is to incorporate it into the design.

The collection of some 500 rules, principles, and maxims that follows includes insight into the laws governing important matters such as supermarket lines, pizza delivery, diaper management, houseplant morbidity, dieting, car repair, and the tendencies of inanimate objects such as telephones and socks in pairs.

If there is a central theme to this work it is summed up in *Gumperson's Law:* The probability of anything happening is in inverse ratio to its desirability.

This law is central to most homes today and should be explained. It first appeared in the November 1957 issue of *Changing Times* magazine and was credited to a Dr. R. F. Gumperson. It was printed in conjunction with an article on firewood, to account for that phenomenon known to anyone who has tried to light a fire in a fireplace or outdoor grill, to wit: "that you can throw a burnt match out the window of your car and start a forest fire, while you can use two boxes of matches and a whole edition of the Sunday paper without being able to start a fire under the dry logs in your fireplace."

Gumperson was a pioneer in the field of diviscism, the science of making predictions according to the law of diverges (a diverge being the opposite of an average). Over time, Gumperson was able to use diviscism to prove other important phenomena, such as that the person buying the most lottery tickets has the least chance of winning; or that after a raise in salary you will have less money at the end of each month than you had before; and the fact that good parking spaces are always on the other side of the street.

Research has subsequently shown that Gumperson was really John W. Hazard, who was the editor of *Changing Times* magazine. This in no way diminishes the discoveries that carry Gumperson's name or those findings created by his disciples, such as yours truly, who is fascinated by the fact that so many people believe they can win those massive publishers' sweepstakes but will never be hit by lightning. The late H. Allen Smith, who once wrote that he thought Gumperson's law was written just for him, came up with many proofs of it, my favorite being that a rattle in your car will disappear as soon as a mechanic starts listening for it.

All of the laws that follow appear in the exact language of the people who discovered the phenomenon or universal truth, including their name for that discovery. Every attempt has been made to find the original author of each discovery, but sadly, some appear as "unknown origin."

The items were collected over a period of years and are listed alphabetically by name to reflect the categorical and chronological randomness that approximates life in most homes.

In addition to the main body of the book, there is a special bonus section from The Murphy Center that, it is hoped, will reopen the national debate on the need to revamp the maxims of everyday life.

A

- **Abby's Formula.** If you want your children to turn out well, spend twice as much time with them and half as much money.
  —Abigail Van Buren,
  Alexandria, Virginia *Journal*,
  May 24, 1995

- **Abercrombie's Theory of Parallel Universe.** There exists a parallel universe into which all our lost objects are sucked, never to be seen again.
  —Denis Abercrombie; from
  Larry Groebe

- **Abley's Explanation.** Marriage is the only union that cannot be organized. Both sides think they are management.
  —William J. Abley,
  Kamloops, B.C., Canada

- **Achilles' Biological Findings.** (1) If a child looks like his father, that's heredity. If he looks like a neighbor, that's environment. (2) A

lot of time has been wasted arguing over who came first—the chicken or the egg. It was undoubtedly the rooster.
> —The late Ambassador
> Theodore C. Achilles,
> Washington, D.C.

• **ACW's Theorems of Practical Physics.**
The volume times the frequency of the neighboring dog's bark is inversely proportional to the intelligence of its owner.
> —Ashley C. Worsley, Baton
> Rouge, Louisiana

• **Addis's Wisdom.** (1) What mindless drivel goes unsaid when teenagers say "like, ya know" instead. (2) No paper bag can hold all the garbage produced by the groceries that came into the house in it. (3) Relativity: It only seems like an eternity between the time a glass is empty and the time the kid stops going "guuu-urk" with the straw. (4) No human on earth can refold a road map, but some excellent origami and paper airplanes have resulted from the effort. (5) If there were only one wrong way to wire your VCR to the TV, you would find it on the first try. (6) I drink—therefore rye am. (7) Nobody will leave you alone—until you want company. (8) A magazine that travels thousands of miles in the care of the Postal Service will wait until you bring it in the house to drop its loose subscription cards on the floor. (9) If the instructions on the childproof cap say to push down hard while twisting, the contents is arthritis medicine. If it can only be opened by tearing at it with your teeth, it's denture cream. (10) The chief advantage of *Homo sapiens* getting up on two feet was that they then could distinguish their dogs from their children. (11) Infinity is nature's way of putting things off. (12) The only time you'll know what people really think of your beard is after you've shaved it off. (13) Life is not too short; it's too narrow. (14) There's nothing that can happen on a football field that can't be described with a cliché. (15) After you have been submitted to toilet training, every act of rebellion is anticlimactic. (16) A barking dog never bites, but he may stop barking at any moment. (17) He who takes comfort in the overwhelming odds against being hit by lightning will be convinced the same odds cannot prevent him from winning the lottery. (18) *Addis's Feline Discovery*. You will never see a cat obedience school.

> —Don Addis, cartoonist and columnist for the *St. Petersburg Times*, whose first rule of humor is "If you're going to joke—be funny."

• **Agel's Law of Tennis Doubles in Which a Husband and Wife Are on the Same Side.** Whenever the husband poaches on his wife's side of the court and shouts, "I've got it, I've got it," you can safely bet that he doesn't.
>—Jerome Agel, *New York Times*, July 30, 1980

• **Mrs. Albert's Law.** If the house is neat, it doesn't have to be clean.
>—Forwarded by Dr. Bernard L. Albert, Scarsdale, New York

• **Alden's Laws.** (1) Giving away baby clothes and furniture is a major cause of pregnancy. (2) Always be backlit. (3) Sit down whenever possible.
>—Nancy Alden, Drexel Hill, Pennsylvania

• **Alexander's Household Laws.** (1) When you need to look up a phone number you will only have the phone book with the other half of the alphabet. (2) If the wife is happy about the toilet seat, the husband should spend more time at home.
>—Paul Alexander, Venice, California

• **Alicia's Discovery.** When you move something to a more logical place, you only can remember where it used to be and your decision to move it.

> —Alicia K. Dustira, New
> Haven, Connecticut

• **Alida's Rule.** The larger the house, the more likely the addition.

> —Alida Kane, Washington,
> D.C.

• **Allen's Lament.** Everybody wants to be waited on.

> —Mary Allen, McLean,
> Virginia

• **Anjard's Teen Theorem.** Their mouths grow disproportionate to their height.

> —Dr. Ron Anjard, Kokomo,
> Indiana

• **Anon's Dietary Law.** The fat you eat is the fat you wear.

> —Bob Norris, Palma de
> Majorca, Spain

• **Anthony's Law of Force.** Don't force it, get a larger hammer.

—Unknown origin

• **Anthony's Law of the Workshop.** Any tool, when dropped, will roll into the least accessible corner of the workshop. *Corollary:* On the way to the corner, any dropped tool will first always strike your toes.

—Unknown origin

• **Apartment Dweller's Law.** One person's floor is another person's ceiling.

—Unknown origin; collected from a radio call-in show

• **Arden's Rules.** (1) A new driver's license means you will move. (2) Transferring the stuff from your old dilapidated address book into a neat, legible, new address book means all your friends will move. (3) If you lose your wallet, it will have more money in it than it has in the past five years.

—Lynne Arden, Oakland, California

• **Avery's Rule of Three.** Trouble strikes in series of threes, but when working around the house the next job after a series of three is not the fourth job—it's the start of a brand-new series of three.

—The fictitious Avery is H. Allen Smith's neighbor in Smith's epic 1960 work on suburban life, *Let the Crabgrass Grow.* Avery is also known for coming up with the saying "There's such a thing as too much point on a pencil."

B

• **Badger's Rule.** Manners are the noises you don't make when eating soup.
> —Joseph E. Badger, Bloomington, Illinois

• **Bailey's Law of the Kinked Helix.** A telephone cord hangs freely with no kinks only in television shows.
> —Kent Bailey, Vienna, Virginia

• **Bair's Rule of Lightning.** Fuses never blow during daylight hours. *Corollary:* Only after the fuses blow do you discover the flashlight batteries are dead and you're out of candles, or matches, or both.
> —Penny Bair, Austin, Texas

• **Ballweg's Discovery.** Whenever there is a flat surface, someone will find something to put on it.
> —Col. Lawrence H. Ballweg, USAF [Retired], Albuquerque, New Mexico

• **Bell's Rules.** (1) The average time between throwing something away and needing it badly is two weeks. This time can be reduced to one week by retaining the thing for a long time first. (2) Linear objects (such as wire, string, etc.), when left to their own devices, occupy time by twisting themselves into tangles and weaving knots. (3) Tiny objects, when dropped, run and hide. (4) There is an updraft over wastebaskets.

> —Norman R. Bell, Associate Professor of Engineering, North Carolina State University

• **Benchley's Travel Distinction.** In America there are two classes of travel—first class, and with children.

> —Robert Benchley

• **Bennett's Laws of Horticulture.** (1) Houses are for people to live in. (2) Gardens are for plants to live in. (3) There is no such thing as a houseplant. *Bennett's Law of the Do-It-Yourself Movement.* Every job you tackle turns out to be seven times more bloody awkward than it ought to be.

> —H. Bennett, West Midlands, England

- **Berliner's Law of Mineral Propagation.**
Wire coat hangers multiply in dark closets.
> —The late Josephine Mitchell
> Berliner, Washington, D.C.,
> from her daughter Joie
> Vargas, Reno, Nevada

- **Billings's Advice** (a smattering). (1) There
are two things in this life for which we are fully
prepared, and that is: twins. (2) Live within your
income even if you have to borrow to do so.
(3) Never work before breakfast; if you have to
work before breakfast, get your breakfast first.
> —American humorist Josh
> Billings, 1918–85

- **Blackwell's Impossibilities.** (1) You cannot tighten one shoelace without tightening the
other one. (2) A true gardener cannot pull just
one weed.
> —Alexander W. Blackwell,
> Pebble Beach, California

- **Blattenberger's Marital Principle.**
Marriages are like union contracts in that six
weeks after the fact, both parties feel that they
could have done better if they had held out a little longer.
> —Larry A. Blattenberger,
> Martinsburg, Pennsylvania

- **Blay's Discovery.** Long-playing recordings scratch, pop, click, wobble, and warp in direct proportion to the value placed on them by their owner. Hated recordings have built-in damage inhibitors that only self-destruct when the record is passed on to a loving recipient.
  —Robert E. Blay, Rutland, Vermont

- **Bombeck's Principles.** (1) A pregnancy will never occur when you have a low-paying job that you hate. (2) An ugly carpet will last forever.
  —Erma Bombeck, from her column of January 10, 1978

- **Boston's Irreversible Law of Clutter.** In any household, junk accumulates to fill the space available for its storage.
  —Bruce O. Boston, Fairfax, Virginia

- **Boyle's Law.** The first pull on the cord will always send the drapes the wrong way.
  —Charles P. Boyle, Annapolis, Maryland

• **Brattman's Hobby Rule.** After you have purchased the most expensive piece of equipment your hobby requires, you will soon tire of the whole thing.

—Steven Ronald Brattman, Los Angeles, California

• **Breider's Rules.** (1) Inertia has its own momentum. (2) Bodies age, emotions don't. (3) Bad weather lasts; good weather doesn't. (4) An idea that doesn't work is not creative.

—Alice Breider, Madison, Wisconsin

• **Broome's Domestic Discoveries: Kitchen Equation.** Neatness counts; sloppiness multiplies. **Practice.** Everything gets easier with practice—except getting up in the morning.

—David Broome, Phoenix, Arizona

• **Brothers's Distinction.** The biggest difference between men and boys is the cost of their toys.

—Joyce Brothers, quoted in Bennett Cerf's *The Sound of Laughter*, Doubleday, 1970

• **Bryan's Law of Animal Behavior.** The owner of a dog or cat that bites a veterinarian during a visit to a clinic will invariably state, "Gee, Doc, he's never done that before." *Corollary:* The more serious the injury to the doctor, the more the owner will claim it was the doctor's fault.

> —Douglas Bryan, D.V.M., Springfield, Missouri

• **Buck's Bet.** In a household with children any deck of playing cards will have between thirty-eight and fifty-one cards.

> —Sports broadcaster Jack Buck; from Terry B. Smith, Kirksville, Missouri

• **Bunn's Laws.** (1) No matter what one is going to use it for, the extension cord is always a foot too short. (2) No matter how large your vegetables grow, your neighbor's will be larger.

> —Dean Bunn, Brooklyn Center, Minnesota

• **Burnham's Tenth Law.** If there's no alternative, there's no problem.

> —James Burnham; reported by Charles D. Poe

• **Burns's Flaws.** (1) You always discover you're out of toothpaste the morning of your dental appointment. (2) Your sons will remember to put the toilet seat lid down only in public rest rooms. (3) Children acquire an ear for good music only after they have suffered a hearing loss at rock concerts. (4) A child will forget to change his socks only when you take him shopping for new shoes. (5) A teenager will only return your car with a full tank of gas when he's had a fender bender.

> —Catherine Burns, Winslow, Maine

• **Burton's Party Laws.** (1) Any birthday party of more than seven male children under the age of eleven will inevitably end in a fight. (2) Any child's birthday party in which the number of guests exceeds the number of the actual age of the child for whom the party is being given will end in disaster.

> —Abbreviated list of party laws by Pierre Burton, from his book *My War With the 20th Century,* Doubleday, 1965

- **Buxbaum's Law.** Anytime you back out of your driveway or parking lot, day or night, there will always be a car coming, or a pedestrian walking by.

> —Unknown origin; from Jack Womeldorf

- **Buxbaum's Rule.** Nothing stimulates interest in foreign affairs like having a son of military age.

> —Martin Buxbaum, quoted in Bill Gold's column, *Washington Post*, May 6, 1981

- **Byron's Tart Caveat to the Voyager.** Wives in their husband's absences grow subtler, and daughters sometimes run off with the butler.

> —Don Widener, in his biography of Jack Lemmon, *Lemmon;* from Barry Hugh Yeakle, North Manchester, Indiana

C

• **Callie's Law of Dinner Preparedness.**
When the smoke alarm goes off, dinner is
served.

> —Caroline Curtis, Falls
> Church, Virginia

• **Campbell's Constant.** The telephone never
rings until you are settled in the bathroom.

> —Constance E. Campbell,
> Keokuk, Iowa. An alternative
> version, Stinton's Law, holds
> that "the telephone bell is
> connected to the toilet seat."
> This law was discovered by
> Genie Stinton of Cypress,
> California.

• **Carlisle's Nursing Keystone.** If you treat a
sick child like an adult and a sick adult like a
child, everything works out pretty well.

> —Ruth Carlisle, quoted in
> *Reader's Digest*, January 1969

• **Carlisle's Rule of Acquisition.** The purchase of any product can be rationalized if the desire to own it is strong enough.
—Carlisle Madson, Hopkins, Minnesota

• **Caroline's First Law of Housekeeping.** Every flat surface is a table.
—Caroline Laudig-Herschel, Mountain View, California

• **Carpenter's Discovery.** The usefulness of an item ends when you throw it away.
—Dan Carpenter, Indianapolis, Indiana

• **Carter's Rule.** If there is a single puddle in your front yard, the newsboy will hit it, but only on those days when the paper is unwrapped.
—Nelson Carter, Aptos, California

• **Carvlin's Commentary.** In marriage, a warm heart seldom compensates for cold hands.
—Tom Carvlin, Dolton, Illinois

• **Cher's Matrimonial Analogy.** Husbands are like fires. They go out when unattended.
>—Actress Cher, quoted in the *National Enquirer,* August 22, 1983; from Bernard L. Albert

• **Christmas Eve, The Primary Myth of.** "So simple that a child can assemble it."
>—Side panel of a toy box that also says, "Some assembly required."

• **Christmas Morning, The First Discovery of.** Batteries not included.
>—From the side panel of a toy box; small print

• **Churchill's Marital Admission.** My wife and I tried two or three times in the last forty years to have breakfast together, but it was so disagreeable we had to stop.
>—Winston Churchill, quoted in *Forbes,* June 30, 1986

• **Clark's First Law of Relativity.** No matter how often you trade dinner or other invitations with in-laws, you will lose a small fortune in the exchange. *Corollary:* Don't try it; you cannot drink enough of your in-laws' booze to get even before the liver fails.

> —Jackson Clark, Cuero,
> Texas, to Alan Otten

• **Claudia's Warning.** Anything small enough to fit in a pocket will eventually end up in the washing machine.

> —Claudia H. Sundman,
> Eaton, New Hampshire, who
> noted this with the submis-
> sion: "I first realized the rule
> while sailing as Purser on the
> S.S. *Ocean Phoenix,* a factory
> ship with a crew of 200. The
> captain asked me why our
> billet cards (which note
> duties for Emergency and
> Life Boat drills and are about
> the size of a credit card) kept
> ending up in the laundry."

• **Collins's Law of Economics.** The cost of living will always rise to exceed income.

> —Roger W. Collins, St. Louis,
> Missouri; from Elaine Viets

• **Col. Tengen's Law.** If you're really in a hurry, avoid the express checkout lines; the cashiers will be exchanged as soon as you're next in line for service.
> —Col. James T. Tengen,
> Rancho Palos Verde,
> California

• **Corcoran's Laws** (on visiting people who own a poodle). (1) Never visit people who own a poodle. (2) If you do visit people who own a poodle, never throw a ball or small squeak toy to the poodle if you wish to be left alone during the remainder of the visit.
> —John H. Corcoran, Jr., tele-
> vision personality and critic
> extraordinaire, Los Angeles,
> California

• **Covert Conversation Rule.** If you don't want your children to hear what you are saying, pretend you're talking to them.
> —Anonymous

• **Crane's Rule.** There are three ways to get something done: do it yourself, hire someone, or forbid your kids to do it.
> —Monta Crane, in *Sunshine*
> magazine and requoted in
> *Reader's Digest,* June 1977

• **Cripps's Law.** When traveling with children on one's holidays, at least one child of any number of children will request a rest-room stop exactly halfway between any two given rest areas.

> —Mervyn Cripps, St. Catherines, Ontario, Canada in a letter to *Verbatim*

• **Crisp's Creed.** Don't keep up with the Joneses. Drag them down, it's cheaper.

> —Quentin Crisp; from Richard Isaac, M.D., Toronto, Ontario, Canada

D

- **Daum's Law of Cuckoo Clocks.** At any given party, the cuckoo will always cuckoo at the most embarrassing moment in a conversation.

>—Michael J. Daum, East Chicago, Indiana

- **Davis's Discovery.** If you want to start a bug collection, paint your lawn furniture.

>—Lee A. Davis, Wilmington, Delaware

- **Davison's Law.** One allows to come to rest any sizable object—laundry basket, grocery bag, shoes, etc.—in the exact location that impedes as much foot traffic as possible.

>—Unknown origin from W. Harper Girvin, Charlottesville, Virginia

- **DeBleyker's Discovery.** Forgetting is a poor excuse for not remembering.

>—J. R. DeBleyker, Lyndhurst, Ohio

- **Debrokowski's Laundry Law.** If you come out of the Laundromat with an even number of socks, you have somebody else's laundry.

> —Unknown origin; collected from a radio call-in show. There are many laws about socks, but Debrokowski's may be the most immutable.

- **Dickson's Gardening Discovery.** When weeding, the best way to make sure what you are pulling is a weed and not a valuable plant is to pull on it. If it come out of the ground easily, it is a valuable plant.

> —Paul Dickson, Director for Life, The Murphy Center

- **Dickson's Rules.** *Insomnia.* (1) Noises, particularly drips and creakings, intensify during the night but abate at dawn. (2) Birds make the most noise at dawn. (3) At the *precise moment* that you *must* get out of bed, there will be absolute quiet. *Suburban Development.* The more trees a developer cuts down, the woodsier the name of the resulting housing development.

> —Paul Dickson, Director for Life, The Murphy Center

• **Disney World Rule.** Children under twelve must be accompanied by money.
> —James Dent, Charleston, West Virginia, *Gazette*

• **Dr. Griffitts's Discovery.** Pride is no match for dirty diapers.
> —James J. Griffitts, M.D., Dunnellan, Florida

• **Dr. Hayes's Hint.** Helpful hints aren't.
> —Brian E. Hayes, M.D., Rosebud, Oregon

• **Dolan's Query.** Did your wife ever get a permanent? Where is it now?
> —Postcard from Wayne Dolan, seventy-seven, of Raytown, Missouri

• **Dorothy's Dilemma.** The heavier the package and the farther you must carry it—the more your nose itches.
> —Dorothy Delphous, Garden Grove, California

• **Doudna's Given.** Whenever you tell someone what you paid for something you bought, you find out either (a) where you could have bought the same thing cheaper, or (b) where you

could have bought something better for the
same price.

> —Paul Doudna, Ferguson,
> Missouri

• **Dunn's Dally on Doing.** Never do now
what must be done or you may not find anything to do when you are looking for something
to do later.

• **Dunn's Observation.** If all the telephone
calls from firms claiming that they are in the
neighborhood installing siding, solar heat, roof-
ing, carpeting, basement waterproofing, insula-
tion, kitchen cabinets, patios, storm windows,
rec rooms, bathroom tile, etc., were true, the
city would need massive around-the-clock traffic
control on my street so they could get another
car down the street to give me my free estimate
"as long as they are in the neighborhood."

> —The late Russell J. Dunn,
> Sr., Lakewood, Ohio

• **Dwyer's Law of Pins.** If you unwrap a new
article of clothing that is secured by n pins, you
will remove $n - 1$ pins. And that pin will pierce
you in a place that hurts.

> —Edward J. Dwyer, Cherry
> Hill, New Jersey

• **Dyer's Discovery.** The basic fine print for all insurance policies says, "This policy is void in case of a claim."
—Frederick C. Dyer,
Somerset, Maryland

• **Dykema's One-on-One Law.** Your house makes strange noises only when you are alone.
—Denise Dykema, Morrison, Illinois

E

• **Ear's Law.** Before a party or a trip, if it can, it will let rip.

> —From the column "Ear" in the late *Washington Star.* It was recalled in print when Jimmy and Rosalynn Carter's hot-water heater burst on their last day in Plains before leaving for the inauguration.

• **Elliott's Household Rules.** (1) No matter when you start, bedtime happens at 11:30 P.M. (2) There's no such thing as a "long winter evening," since none of the chores saved for a long winter evening ever get done. (3) All clocks in the house conspire to display totally different readings. (4) The cat never goes out the door the first time you open it.

> —Owen Elliott, Ridgefield, Connecticut

• **Ellis's Reciprocal.** An unwatched pot boils immediately. *Corollary:* The speed with which boiling milk rises from the bottom of the pan to any point beyond the top is greater than the speed at which the human brain and hand can combine to snatch the wretched thing off.

> —H. F. Ellis, "Men in Aprons," *Punch*; from Ross Reader

• **Epperson's Law.** When a man says it's a silly, childish game, it's probably something his wife can beat him at.

> —Don Epperson, quoted in Bill Gold's "District Line" column in the *Washington Post*, September 11, 1978

• **Eve's Discovery.** At a bargain sale, the only suit or dress that you like best and that fits is the one not on sale. *Adam's Corollary:* It's easy to tell when you've got a bargain—it doesn't fit.

> —Fred Dyer, Somerset, Maryland

F

- **Family Law.**
    Where there's a sibling
    There's quibbling.
    > —Selma Raskin. It originally
    > appeared in the *Wall Street
    > Journal* and is quoted in
    > Charles Preston's *The Light
    > Touch.*

- **Feline Frustration, Rule of.** When your
cat has fallen asleep on your lap and looks utter-
ly content and adorable, you will suddenly have
to go to the bathroom.
    > —Unknown origin; from
    > Donald R. Woods

• **Finagle's Proofs, Household Examples.**
(1) Any vacuum cleaner would sooner take the
nap off a rug than remove white threads from a
dark rug. (2) No dog will knock a vase over
unless it has water in it.

> —From a collection of
> "Finagle's Laws" published in
> *Astounding Science Fiction* in
> the late 1950s

• **Fischer's Findings.** Sex is hereditary. If
your parents never had it, chances are you won't
either.

> —Joseph Fischer, West
> Melbourne, Florida; from the
> August 1974 *Harper's* maga-
> zine

• **Forbes's Rule of Parenting.** Let your children go if you want to keep them.

> —Malcolm Forbes, *The
> Sayings of Chairman Malcolm*,
> Harper & Row, 1978

• **Foster's Law.** Children will always have to
go to the bathroom as soon as you sit down in a
restaurant.

> —Marguerite H. Foster, Palo
> Alto, California

• **Frank's First Law of Fluid Dynamics.**
The greatest amount of effort exerted by a
homeowner on his plumbing will produce the
least amount of results. *Frank's Second Law of
Fluid Dynamics.* The least amount of effort
exerted by a homeowner on his plumbing will
produce the greatest amount of water.
> — Frank Johnson, Sterling,
> Virginia

• **Fred's Forecast.** Golf is like children.
They're both humbling experiences waiting to
happen.
> — Fred Whistle, North
> Barrington, Illinois

• **Fullner's Rule of Weekends.** Whenever
the only time available to complete a task is on
weekends, all suppliers of necessary parts, mate-
rial, and equipment will be open for business
Monday through Friday.
> —Randall Fullner, San Jose,
> California

G

- **Gannon's Theory of Relativity.**
Grandchildren grow more quickly than children.
—William P. Gannon,
Glenolden, Pennsylvania

- **Gardening, Laws of.** (1) Other people's
tools work only in other people's yards. (2)
Fancy gizmos don't work. (3) If nobody uses it,
there's a reason. (4) You get the most of what
you need the least.
—Jane Bryant Quinn, in her
newspaper column syndicated
by the *Washington Post*, 1975

- **Geist's Basic Rule for Travel with Kids.**
Never in the same direction.
—William E. Geist, *New York
Times*, October 10, 1982

- **Gilbert's Discovery.** Any attempts to use
any of the new super glues results in the two
pieces sticking to your thumb and index finger
rather than each other.
—Mike Gilbert, Santa Ana,
California

GEIST'S BASIC RULE
FOR TRAVEL

• **Glanville's Observations.** The more fragile the product, the higher it will be placed in a coin-operated machine.

—Bradley Glanville, Chico, California

• **Graditor's Laws.** (1) If it can break, it will, but only after the warranty expires. (2) A necessary item only goes on sale after you have purchased it at the regular price.

—Sherry Graditor, Skokie, Illinois

• **Graham's Law of Plumbing.** He who bathes last bathes fastest.

—Charles Graham, The Mount, Oxford Road, Gerrards Cross, Bucks, U.K.

• **Gumperson's Law of Childhood.** Children have more energy after a hard day of play than they do after a good night's sleep.

> —Attributed to Dr. R. F. Gumperson in the November 1957 issue of *Changing Times*. The actual author of this law and the basic law that follows was the magazine's editor, John W. Hazard.

• **Gumperson's Law.** The probability of anything happening is in inverse ratio to its desirability.

• **Gustafson's Advice.** Anything you look for in the Yellow Pages will not be listed in the category you first try to find it under. Start with the second.

> —John W. Gustafson, San Francisco, California

GWEN'S LAW

• **Gwen's Law.** Do not join encounter groups. If you enjoy being made to feel inadequate, call your mother.

> —Liz Smith, from *The Mother Book,* Doubleday, 1978

H-I

• **Hagan's Law of Tool Placement.** It's in the other room.

> —Jim Hagan; from W. E. McKean II

• **Hall's Law of Vehicular Noise.** There is an inverse relationship between the intelligence of the driver and the noise made by the driver's vehicle.

> —Donald M. Hall, Radford, Virginia

• **Halperin's Laundry Rule.** All lingerie put in the washer inside out comes out of the washer inside out. All lingerie put in the washer right side out comes out inside out.

> —Judith Halperin, Chicago, Illinois

• **Harkness's Discovery.** The harder it is to stay awake on the drive home, the harder it will be to fall asleep when you get there.

> —R. J. Harkness, Ruth, California

• **Hauser's Truth.** If you have a garden wedding, the cesspool runs over.
> —Georgia Hauser, Albion,
> California

• **Haviland's Discoveries.** (1) *Observations of False Alarms:* The smoke detector battery will always run out in the night, causing it to start beeping. (2) *Dieter's Despair:* There are more food commercials on TV when you are on a diet. (3) *Time's Truth:* You do not necessarily have to be having fun for time to fly. (4) *Linear Reality:* There is a fine line between pessimism and realism. (5) *Law of Firsts:* The first time you do, you shouldn't have. The first time you don't, you should have. (For example, the first time you *do* run that stop sign because "there's never anything coming the other way," there will be and it will be the police. The first time you *don't* ask if there is anything you can pick up at the store is the day you come home and find there is no bathroom tissue in the house.)
> —James D. Haviland, Halifax,
> Nova Scotia, Canada

• **Hebert's Laws.** (1) *The Law of Natural Compensation:* Any stroke of unexpected good fortune will be compensated for, within forty-eight hours, by 1.22 strokes of misfortune.

Corollary: If the checkbook has extra funds, something expensive will go wrong with the car. (2) *First Law of Notification:* Snoring is nature's way of telling you that your spouse is still in the bed. (3) *First and Only Law of Complaints:* Don't complain. The people who will listen can't do anything about it, while the people who can do something about it won't listen. (4) *Hebert's Safe Places Observation:* You are never as clever in locating the thing you put in a "safe place" as you were when putting it there.

—John M. Hebert, New
Baltimore, Michigan

• Helen's Inanimate Object Lessons.
(1) The certainty of an object's loss is directly related to the "specialness" of the place you put it. (2) If you buy a new one, the old one will turn up (90 percent probability). *The Cognitive Corollary:* The more confident you are of remembering, the more likely you are to forget. *The Bonus Intuitive Rule of Object Placement:* Once you finally find an object, put it in the first place you thought to look for it, particularly if you returned to that place more than once in your search. Do NOT apply any other rule of logic to this choice. Do NOT choose a place that seems in any way "special."

—From John A. Mattsen,
Finlayson, Minnesota, who

also brought this set of laws
to the attention of The
Murphy Center:

• **Helen's Rule of the Two-Year-Old.**
(1) They will never tell you that they have to go
to the bathroom. . . (2) until after you have
dressed them in boots, mittens, coat, snow
pants, scarf, and hat. (3) By the time you
undress them, it's too late. (4) If it's not too late,
it was a false alarm. (5) If it was a false alarm
the first time, it won't be a false alarm once you
get them dressed again.

> —From John A. Mattsen,
> Finlayson, Missouri

• **Hill's Pet Law.** The life expectancy of tropical fish is in direct, but opposite, proportion to
their purchase price. *Corollary:* Expensive
breeds of dogs always run away and get lost;
mongrels never do.

> —Pierre Allen Hill, York,
> Pennsylvania

• **Hirabayashi's First Law of Housekeeping.**
There is no convenient time for the cat to throw
up on the carpet.

> —Judy Hirabayashi, Oakland,
> California

• **Holliday's Discovery.** If lonely, sort laundry, get out the vacuum cleaner, put trash bags inside the door, and company will arrive.
> —Philip Holliday, North Webster, Indiana

• **Home Buyer's Rule.** The house you want is two steps above the house you can afford.
> —Jane O'Callahan, realtor, San Jose, California

• **Hood's Employment Rules.** Never hire a plumber who wears rubber boots or an electrician who has scorched eyebrows.
> —Bob Hood, writing in the March 14, 1993, *Fort Worth Telegram*

• **Hopkins's Baby Law.** Much of what goes in must come out, but not necessarily by the expected route.
> —C. M. Hopkins, Berkshire, England

• **Horton's Maxims.** (1) Nature always wins. (2) Nothing is waterproof.
> —Scott Horton, San Francisco, California

• **Howard's Comparison.** Permitting your life to be taken over by another person is like letting the waiter eat your dinner.

> —Vernon Howard; from Bob Heimberg, Las Vegas, Nevada

• **Howe's Verities.** Families with babies, and families without babies, are so sorry for each other.

> —E. W. Howe, from his *Country Town Sayings,* 1911

• **Hubbard's Household Credos.** (1) The fellow who owns his own home is always just coming out of the hardware store. (2) The fellow that brags about how cheaply he heats his home always sees the first robin. (3) We all like our relatives when we're little. (4) To stop dandruff there is nothing like blue serge. (5) Onions speak louder than words. (6) There is somebody at every dinner party who eats all the celery.

> —Frank McKinney "Kin" Hubbard (1859–1915), humorist and cartoonist, from various sources. All of these were uttered by Hubbard's fictional alter ego, Abe Martin.

- **Immutability, Two Rules of.** (1) If a small boy can get dirty, he will. (2) If a teenager can go out, he/she will.

> —Anonymous, in the *Robbins Reader,* a 1980 issue

- **Inlander's Theory of Relativity.**
Everybody has relatives.

> —Charlie Inlander, Allentown, Pennsylvania; from Steve Stine. Bill McFadin of Jacksonville, Florida, on seeing Inlander's Theory, has come up with *McFadin's Southern Supplement,* which holds: If you live in Florida and have northern relatives, they will visit. Often. And complain about how far you are from the beach and Walt Disney World.

- **Irreversible Law of the Toe Holes.** No matter which side of the sock a hole is in, you will always put the sock on so that your big toe protrudes through the hole.

> —Tom Eddins, Harding University, Searcy, Arkansas

J

• **Jackson's Laws.** Shopping centers are for people who don't have to go to the bathroom.
> —Michael Jackson, KABC Radio, Los Angeles, California

• **Jake's Law.** Anything hit with a big enough hammer will fall apart.
> —Robert A. "Jake" Jackson, Socorro, New Mexico

• **Jane's Gospel.** When there are two or more identical articles to be built or repaired, difficulty will be encountered, but only while attempting to build or repair the second (or last) one. *Corollary 1:* When both the hot and cold water faucets are leaking, the knob of the first one will be removed, the washer replaced, and the knob put back on with no complications. While attempting to repair the second, however, one will encounter (a) a permanently welded knob, (b) a screw head stripped bare, (c) a knob that fit until removed but cannot possibly be

reused, or (d) all of the above. *Corollary 2:* If the
first article is dismantled again in order to
determine why it went back together so easily, it
will not.

—Jane L. Hassler, Marina del
Rey, California

• **Jaroslovsky's Law.** The distance you have to
park from your apartment increases in proportion to the weight of packages you're carrying.

—Unknown origin; from Alan
Otten

• **Jason's Law.** An unbreakable toy is good
for breaking other toys.

—Bruce W. Van Roy, Vienna,
from the "Style Invitational,"
Washington Post, July 10,
1994

• **Jerri's Law.** If I have a nickel, I'll spend a dime.

> —Jerri Locke, Fort Worth, Texas

• **Jewell's Rule of Domestic Horticulture.** The probability of grass growing in any given spot is inversely proportional to one's desire to have it there.

> —History Professor Fred R. Jewell, Harding University, Searcy, Arkansas, who formulated the rule one day "while pulling sizable outcroppings of grass from the cracks in my driveway and simultaneously noting the bare spots in my lawn just a few feet away"

• **Jim's Rule.** The rental of any apartment in a major city will guarantee that the building will go condo.

> —Unknown origin, WIND Radio

• **Jinny's Sister's Legacy.** Be careful what you give people as gifts; you may get them back when they die.

> —Margaret W. Carpenter, Marshall L. Smith Collection

• **Johnson's Law.** The amount of tears produced in a man's eyes while he is cutting onions is directly proportional to the amount of women gathered to watch him.

> —Carleton E. Johnson,
> Department of State,
> Washington, D.C.

• **Jolliffe's Rules for Parents.** (1) After all have reached agreement, regardless of the bicycle you eventually buy your child, the next-door neighbor's kid will be given the one your child really wanted after all. (2) The amount of time a child plays with a new Christmas toy is always one-fifth of the time it took for the parent to assemble it.

> —Richard K. Jolliffe,
> Saskatoon, Saskatchewan,
> Canada

• **Joyce's Law of Bathroom Hooks.** A bathroom hook will be loaded to capacity immediately upon becoming available.

> —John Joyce, Waldie and
> Briggs Inc., Chicago, Illinois;
> from Alan Otten. According
> to Joyce, there is more to this
> law than immediately meets
> the eye, as it "applies to free-
> ways, closets, playgrounds,

downtown hotels, taxis, parking lots, bookcases, wallets, purses, pockets, pipe racks, basement shelves, and so on. The list is endless." However, he is the first to concede that further research is called for. As he told Otten in a note, "The ultimate test of the law, which I have been postponing, would be to array hooks in a continuous strip around the bathroom to see if the towels, bathrobes, etc., actually meet in the middle of the room, preventing opening of the door and entry of would-be bathers."

• **Jump's Discovery.** One of the great mysteries of life is how the idiot your daughter married can be the father of the smartest grandchildren in the world.

—Gary Jump, Bensenville, Illinois

K

- **Kae's Law.** Changing the baby's diaper causes the phone to ring.

—Kae Evensen Marty,
Sacramento, California

- **Kaplan's Dictum.** If you are unable to decide between two things, do whichever is cheapest.

—Unknown origin; Fred
Bondy, Wilmette, Illinois

- **Kaplan's Law of the Instrument.** Give a small boy a hammer and he will find that everything he encounters needs pounding.

—Abraham Kaplan

- **Kara McVey's Law.** If you are having a good hair day, you won't have anywhere to go.

—Kara McVey, Waynesville,
Missouri

- **Karen's Constant.** If a small object is dropped in the bathroom, it will go down the drain. A large object falls into the toilet.

—Karen Statzel, Kirkwood,
Missouri

KARA M°VAY'S LAW

• **Kaul's Collection.** (1) Do not try to solve all life's problems at once—learn to dread each day as it comes. (2) Don't bake cookies; the children will only eat them.

> —Donald Kaul, *Des Moines Register.* These are laws and observations sent to Kaul by readers of his "Over the Coffee" column.

• **Kener's Law.** Tape doesn't stick where (or when) you want it. Tape only sticks to itself.

> —Reed Kener; from Larry Groebe, San Antonio, Texas

• **The Kennedy Law.** If you have a sore toe, care should be exercised in removing your trousers. Do not drop them, or your belt buckle will invariably fall on the sore toe.

> —Wallace Kennedy, Chesterfield, Missouri

• **Kerber's Law on the Inverse Half-Life of Kids' Cars.** Give a kid under twenty-one a first car of any make, model, age, etc. The expected life of that car will be between three weeks and three months. You can double that expected life for any subsequent cars. (It keeps doubling.)
—Robert L. Kerber,
Oceanside, California

• **Kesulab's Law.** Band-Aids stick to children only when they are in traction.
—Gary O. Balusek, Xenia,
Ohio

• **Key to Happiness.** You may speak of love and tenderness and passion, but real ecstasy is discovering you haven't lost your keys after all.
—Clark Kerr, Marshall L.
Smith Collection

- **Kibble's Cat Law.** Cats will only sit in the laps of those who have allergies, hate cats, or both.
>—Gary Kibble, Satellite
>Beach, Florida

- **King's Law of Swimming Pools.** When you build a swimming pool, hire a state highway engineer. They always build highways that hold water.
>—John J. King, Pitts, Georgia

- **Kottmeyer's Ring-Around-the-Tub Principle.** Telephones displace bodies immersed in water.
>—Martin S. Kottmeyer,
>Carlyle, Illinois

- **Kozub's Household Rules.** (1) Super glue isn't. (2) The magazine article you wanted to save is always in last week's trash. (3) Commercially produced art prints are never sized to fit commercially produced frames. (4) Homegrown ice (in your freezer) is never clear. (5) Stick-proof muffin pans aren't. (6) Bathwater is never the right temperature.
>—Fred Kozub, Richmond,
>Virginia

L

• **Lada's Commuter Corollary.** As soon as construction is complete on the fastest, most convenient expressway route from your home to your place of work, you will be transferred to another place of work.
> —Stephen C. Lada, Detroit, Michigan

• **Ladof's Laws of Legal Services.** Most parents, when they demand custody, never seem to remember that it means they get the *kids*.
> —Attorney Anne Ladof, Emigsville, Pennsylvania

• **Landers's Law of the Pinch.** Usually when the shoe fits—it's out of style.
> —Ann Landers, in her column for February 6, 1977

• **Laura's Law.** No child throws up in the bathroom.
> —Unknown origin; from Donald R. Woods

• **Lee's Law.** Mother said there would be days like this, but she never said there'd be so many.

> —Jack Lee, WLAK Radio, Chicago, Illinois

• **Lender's Law.** The law of lending is to break the borrowed article.

> —Unknown origin; collected from a radio call-in show

• **Leslie's Law of Great Expectations.** The richer the relative, the easier it is to remember his or her birthday.

> —Unknown origin; from Arlen Wilson

• **Levin's Law.** Any attempt to adjust the air conditioner will make it worse.

> —Bernard Levin, the *Times* (London), July 9, 1980

• **Lichtenberg's Insights.** The zoning laws in most American neighborhoods would not *permit* the construction of a Parthenon.

> —Benjamin Lichtenberg, Verona, New Jersey, from his book *Insights of an Outsider,* Jaico Publishing, 1972

• **Linda's Law.** The best two hours of sleep start exactly one hour before the alarm clock goes off.

> —Linda Welsch, from "Life Au Naturel" by Roger Welsch in the March 1992 issue of *Natural History*

• **Linda's Law of Teenage Drivers.** If you go where you're not supposed to, the car will break down.

> —Unknown origin; from a radio call-in show, KMOX, St. Louis

• **Lipsett's Law.** You don't know someone until you live with him, but you don't know him well until you divorce him.

> —Donna Lipsett, El Paso, Texas

• **Liston's Law of Gift Wrapping.** No matter how many boxes you save, you will never have one the right size.

> —Jean Liston, Shelby, Ohio

• **Little Doc's Animal Laws.** (1) There is no such thing as a *free* cat. (2) The less a person knows about a breed, the more he will pay for a specimen. (3) The less a person knows about a species (e.g., skunk, ocelot), the more he wants one.

> —Dr. E. S. (Little Doc) Lundgren, Spring Hills, Kansas

• **Loch's Warning.** Read too much self-help literature and you'll need help.

> —Randy Loch, Willingboro, New Jersey

• **Long-Range Planning, The (F)law of.** The longer ahead you plan a special event, and the more special it is, the more likely it is to go wrong.

> —David Evelyn, Arlington, Virginia

• **Lopez's Law of Homework.** Never help your kids with their homework. Getting help with the homework defeats the purpose of education, which is to teach humility.

> —Marsha Lopez, Westmont, Illinois

• **Lowe's Law.** If two pills are required, three pills will come out of the bottle. *Corollary:* When attempting to put the third pill back in the bottle, two pills will go in.

> —Judith Lowe, Hertfordshire, England

• **Lucy's Law of Horizontal Gravity.** Gravity causes any object she drops to disappear under the bed or under the dresser.

> —From Paul S. Humphries, Mishawahn, Indiana, created by his wife, Lucy

M

- **Malik's Observations.** The same piece of tape that would not hold up your child's drawing will not come off the refrigerator.

    —Julia Malik, Richboro, Pennsylvania

- **Marsolais's Laws.** (1) *Diminishing Credibility.* Your trusty dependable lawn mower starts every time on the second pull, the only exception being when you're trying to sell it to your neighbor, at which time twenty-seven pulls are required to start it. (2) *Unfittingness.* No matter which utility company sends you a bill, the envelope they provide for its return to themselves is always one-quarter inch shorter than the bill.

    —Maurice Marsolais, Fairfax, Virginia

- **Martin's Rule.** By the time you run into the house, get the binoculars, and run back outside, the strange bird will have left its perch.

    —Lynn Martin, Mount Laurel, New Jersey

- **Maslow's Maxim.** If the only tool you have is a hammer, you treat everything like a nail.
                    —Abraham Maslow, the
                    noted psychiatrist; from
                    Sydney J. Harris, the noted
                    columnist. It is Harris's
                    "favorite modern saying."

- **McClannahan's Rules of Home Improvement.** (1) Each improvement project begets two more. (2) Each project gets more expensive.
                    —Mike McClannahan,
                    Kansas City, Missouri

- **McConnell's Observation.** The only thing that works in an old house is the owner.
                    —Spero McConnell; from his
                    brother Ray, Miami, Florida

- **McKinnon's Realization.** In real life there is no background music.
                    —Leila A. McKinnon, St.
                    Louis, Missouri

• **Mead's Law of Human Migration.** At least 50 percent of the human race doesn't want their mother-in-law within walking distance.
> —The late Margaret Mead, explaining rural migration to a symposium on the phenomenon. Submitted by Paul Martin via Donald R. Woods.

• **Mendoza's Laws of Purchasing.** (1) When shopping, never look for something specific; you won't find it. (2) Always shop for nothing; you'll always come back with something. (3) After a heavy day's shopping, the perfect purchase is in either the first or the last place you've looked.
> —Liz Mendoza, Fargo, North Dakota

• **Merrill's Maxim of Instant Status.** It is nice to be content in a little house by the side of the road, but a split-level in suburbia is a lot more comfortable.
> —Charles Merrill Smith, from his book *Instant Status, or How to Become a Pillar of the Upper Middle Class,* Doubleday, 1972

• **Mikadet's Cardinal Rule for Parents of Adult Children.** An eighteen-year-old can: (a) vote, (b) rebuild an automobile engine, (c) swallow a guitar pick.

> —T. K. Mikadet, Lompoc, California

• **Miller's Axioms of Outdoor Grilling.** (1) The fire is always at its peak fifteen minutes after dinner. (2) If you overhear the cook saying, "No problem, I'll just dust it off," it's time to visit the salad bowl.

> —Bryan Miller, *New York Times*, June 27, 1984; from Tom Gill

• **Miller's Law.** All costs walk on two legs.
> —Arjay Miller; from Hal Hoverland, Dean, California State College, San Bernardino

• **Mom's Law II.** When they finally do have to take you to the hospital, your underwear won't be new or clean.
> —Dennis Rogers

- **Momma's Rule.** If you can't stand to eat, get out of my kitchen.

> —From the comic strip "Momma" by Mell Lazarus

- **Montgomery's Explanation of the Facts of Life.** All normal young people want to do this thing. It is natural, like fighting.

> —Attributed to Lord Montgomery

- **Morgan's Correlation.** The longer the vacuum cleaner cord, the sooner it gets caught on something.

> —Karen Sorensen Morgan, New York, New York

- **Morris's Laws of Animal Appeal.** The age of a child is inversely correlated with the size of the animals it prefers.

> —Desmond Morris from *The Naked Ape*, McGraw-Hill, 1967

- **Moseley's Truism.** You may not always get what you pay for, but you always pay for what you get.

> —Albert G. Moseley, West Melbourne, Florida

• **Mueth's Law.** Use the last key in the bunch because that's the only one that will unlock the door.

> —Charles J. Mueth, Belleville, Illinois

• **Myers's Observation.** A parent who sends a child to school with the understanding that the child is to call if he is not feeling better should expect a call.

> —Elementary school principal G. E. Myers, Sumpter, South Carolina

N

- **N–1 Law.** If you need four screws for a job, the first three will be easy to find.

  —Unknown origin, WRC Radio

- **Napier's Discovery.** In the past 200 years, America has manufactured close to 100 billion pencils—and we still can't keep one by the phone.

  —Arch Napier, from the *Wall Street Journal*

- **Neudel's Rule for Family Reunions, Large Parties, Meetings, etc.** The person who comes from the farthest distance away always arrives first.

  —Professor Marian Henriquez Neudel, Chicago, Illinois

- **New Laws of Marriage.** (1) Loose change on the bureau is community property. (2) Twice is always (for example, if you forget to take out the garbage twice, you *always* forget to take out the garbage).

  —Anonymous

• **New Parents' Law.** (1) Don't mess with a sleeping baby. (2) Don't mess with a happy baby.

> —Mike McClannahan,
> Kansas City, Missouri. These
> laws are worth the price of
> the book for any parent who
> has ever uttered, "Wouldn't
> you like to see the baby? Let
> me wake him."

• **Nichols's Rule of Success.** Success is when your mother reads about you in the newspaper.

> —Mike Nichols, quoted by
> Henry Hanson in *Chicago*
> magazine, September 1982;
> from Joseph C. Goulden

• **Ninety-Nine Rule of Project Schedules.** The first 90 percent of the task takes 90 percent of the time, the last 10 percent takes the other 90 percent.

> —Commonly heard;
> unknown origin

• **Nolan's Comment on Midlife Crisis.** Sex takes up an infinitesimal amount of one's time, and to have to live with somebody who is listening to this crazy music (e.g., rap) while you want to listen to the Benny Goodman Quartet is a hell of a price to pay for a little sexual pleasure.

> —Dr. William Nolan, quoted by Bob Swift in the *Miami Herald*, January 3, 1987

• **Norden's Law.** You never realize how much furniture you've acquired until you go to the loo in the dark.

> —Dennis Norden on the BBC's "My Word" radio show

• **Norton's Law.** On a cold winter morning your car will have more snow or frost on it than anyone else's.

> —George Norton, Logan, West Virginia

• **Notturno's Discovery.** A bag leaned against the wall will always fall toward you.

> —Peter W. Notturno, Canton, Ohio

O

• **Occam's Electric Razor.** The most difficult lightbulb to replace burns out first and most frequently.

> —Writer Joe Anderson, alluding to fourteenth-century scholar William of Occam and his "Razor," which holds: "Entities ought not to be multiplied except from necessity."

• **Ode (Poem) to a Washer (non-human type).**

Oh, what is so rare, these days of machines
And soap that comes in a box
As a washer and dryer which always return
An even number of sox?

> —Richard M. McBride, La Jolla, California

• **O'Houlihan's Law.** Don't waste your time worrying about rich people, because they sure as heck don't worry about you.

> —Cited in an editorial in the *Alexandria Journal* of August 27, 1991, reacting to the fact that *Regardie's* magazine had pared its list of the area's hundred richest families to seventy-five

• **Old Children's Law.** If it tastes good, you can't have it. If it tastes awful, you'd better clean your plate.

> —"The Wizard," a radio personality, FM 101, Youngstown, Ohio

• **O'Neill's Law of Time Saturation.** The news of the day, no matter how trivial or unimportant, always takes up more time than a married man has. *Corollary:* News stories expand and time contracts, meeting inexorably each day precisely twenty minutes after a man is supposed to be home for dinner.

—Named for Ray O'Neill, who was national affairs editor of the *New York Times*. It was explained in detail in an April 22, 1956, column by James Reston titled "A Note to Miss Truman." Reston quotes Clifton Daniel as having told reporters that his hours at the *Times* were from 9:30 to 5:30. Countered Reston, "It is not a reporter's working hours that count, but the hours he works." He added, "These are regulated by the news, and the news is regulated by a very simple mathematical rule." The rule, of course: *O'Neill's Law.*

- **Olsen's Necktie Law.** The only way to prevent getting food on your necktie is to put it in the refrigerator.

> —Unknown origin: collected from a radio call-in show

- **Osman's Law.** If the plug will only fit into the socket one way, you will always put it in the wrong way first.

> —Charles I. Osman, Hampton, Virginia

- **O'Steen's Rules of Illness.** (1) The germ will keep the child home from work (i.e., school) but not play (i.e., ball game). (2) The opposite is true for adults.

> —Joan O'Steen Hill, Oak Ridge, Tennessee

- **Ozard's Rain Rule.** The amount of rain is directly proportional to the length of time your raincoat is at the dry cleaner.

> —Bill Ozard, Calgary, Alberta, Canada

P

- **Pancoast's Periodical Discovery.** The part of a magazine cover that you especially want to see has been covered with the address label.

    —Charles Pancoast, Akron, Ohio

- **Parent's Law.** By the time you're right, you're dead.

    —Sally Winter, Spring Valley, New York

- **Parson's Laws.** (1) If you break a cup or plate, it will not be the one that was already chipped or cracked. (2) *Parson's Rule.* At whatever stage you apologize to your spouse, the reply is constant—"It's too late now."

    —Denys Parsons, London, England

- **Phelps's Laws of Renovation.** (1) Any renovation project on an old house will cost twice as much and take three times as long as originally estimated. (2) Any plumbing pipes you

choose to replace during renovation will prove
to be in excellent condition; those you decide to
leave in place will be rotten.

> —Lew Phelps, Chicago,
> Illinois; from Alan Otten

• **Pietropinto's Peter Pan Principle.**
Marriages peter out or pan out.

> —Anthony Pietropinto, M.D.,
> in *Husbands and Wives*,
> Times Books, 1979

• **The Pirus Law of Cumulative Clutter.**
Accumulation of old magazines is directly proportional to the cost of the publications and
their relationship to special interests, and
inversely proportional to the number of persons
in the household.

> —Douglas I. Pirus, *Journal of
> Irreproducible Results*, 1988;
> from Norman D. Stevens

• **Pollock's Discovery.** Whichever way you
stand, when you empty the Hoover bag, the dust
always blows in your face.

> —H. M. Pollock, Sevenoaks,
> Kent, England

• **Polsby's Law of Families.** The children of your parents' friends are always nerds.
>—Presidential scholar Nelson Polsby; from Alan Otten

• **The Poorman Flaw.** In any home-improvement project, there will be one mistake so gross that the only solution is to incorporate it into the design.
>—Paul A. Poorman, Akron, who is also responsible for:

• **Poorman's Rule.** When you pull a plastic garbage bag from its handy dispenser package, you always get hold of the closed end and try to pull it open.

• **Pope's Garage Sale Law.** You will get your own junk back in three years. It will cost twice as much. You didn't need it until you sold it. You won't need it after you buy it back.
>—William G. Pope, Somers, New York

• **Porter's Home Rule.** Home is where your garbage is.
>—David Porter; from Ian MacPherson, Regina, Saskatchewan, Canada

• **Preudhomme's Law of Window Cleaning.**
It's on the other side.

> —Unknown origin; from
> Donald R. Woods. In reac-
> tion to this law, Janet M.
> Goldstein of Moylan,
> Pennsylvania, wrote to The
> Murphy Center: "My corol-
> lary—discovered after my
> latest bout with the picture
> window—is: It's not on
> EITHER side."

Q

- **Quality of Life Constant.** Each time in your life when you think you are about to be able to make both ends meet, somebody moves the ends.

> —Unknown origin; collected from a radio call-in show

- **Quirk's Zipper Discovery.** Zippers tend to fail at crucial moments simply because they are treacherous, back-stabbing little fiends.

> —"Dr. Emory Quirk, the Cleveland Institute of Inanimate Hostilities," quoted in a column by Dan Myers, *San Francisco Chronicle*, June 3, 1979

R

- **Rabbe's Rule of the Bedroom.** The spouse (person) that snores the loudest always falls asleep first.

  —Don Rabbe, Lincoln, Nebraska

- **Rappo's Law of Pediatrics.** (1) Children rarely outgrow things they like. (2) Mother's Day is not in May; it's the first day of school.

  —Peter D. Rappo, M.D., Brockton, Massachusetts

- **Raub's Law.** The more expensive the toy, the greater the tendency for the child to play with the box.

  —I. Raub Love, Dayton, Ohio

- **Raufa's Observations.** Earthquake preparedness is a contradiction in terms.

  —Dhyan Raufa, San Francisco, California

• **Rebecca's House Rules** (at least one fits any occasion).

1. Throw it on the bed.
2. Fry onions.
3. Call Jenny's mother.
4. No one's got the corner on suffering.
5. Run it under the cold tap.
6. Everything takes practice, except being born.

—Sharon Mathews,
Arlington, Virginia

• **Reyna McGlone's Discovery.** Lint, dog and cat hair, dirt, dust, etc., are most strongly attracted to objects of opposite color. *Corollary:* There is no such thing as a carpet that doesn't show dirt.

—Augustin Reyna McGlone;
from Don Hall

• **Riberdy's Observations.** (1) Dirty dishes attract surprise visitors. (2) Most swimmers will run for shelter at the first signs of rain. (3) If a picture hangs straight on the first attempt—expect it to fall. (4) Junk mail multiplies if left in the box.

—J. Riberdy, Windsor,
Ontario, Canada

• **Rice's Rule.** No matter when you turn on

the TV, there is always an ad showing.
>—Edith K. Rice, East
>Boothbay, Maine

• **Richman's Inevitables of Parenthood.**
(1) Enough is never enough. (2) The sun always rises in the baby's bedroom window.
(3) Birthday parties always end in tears.
(4) Whenever you decide to take the kids home, it is always five minutes earlier that they break into fights, tears, hysteria.
>—Phillis C. Richman, writer
>and restaurant critic for the
>*Washington Post*

• **Riley's Insurance Realization.** With my luck, nothing will ever happen to me.
>—Chester Riley, played by
>William Bendix, in the "Life
>of Riley" radio show

• **Rippetoe's Motherly Musing.** Parenthood is the only job with a reverse apprenticeship. You start the job with no experience or practical knowledge and total responsibility for a helpless child; as you gain experience and knowledge your responsibility is gradually reduced to practically nothing.
>—Rita Rippetoe, Citrus
>Heights, California

• **Rist's Junk Drawer Discoveries.** (1) All houses have a junk drawer. (2) Anything wanted from the junk drawer will be found at the bottom. (3) Once any item is removed from the junk drawer—no matter how large or small—the junk drawer will not close.

> —Philip Rist, Cleveland, Ohio

• **Robert's Rules of Home and Garden.** (1) If at first you don't succeed, hire a contractor. (2) Two plus two equals four—unless you're talking about inches in a two-by-four. (3) Mulch is ado about nothing. (4) An idle mind should not mess around in a power workshop. (5) We must all hang together or assuredly the pictures will be crooked. (6) Somebody said it couldn't be done. I'll go along with that.

> —Bob Herguth, the *Chicago
> Sun-Times;* from Robert
> Specht

• **Rochester's Theorem.** Before I got married I had six theories about bringing up children; now I have six children and no theories.

> —Lord Rochester

• **Rooney's Law.** You're much more likely to lock a member of your family out of your house than a burglar.

> —Andy Rooney on "60 Minutes"

• **Rose's First Law of Investments.** One should never invest in anything that must be painted or fed.

> —Showman Billy Rose; from William M. Mills, Hutchinson, Kansas

• **Rosenbaum's Rule.** The easiest way to find something lost around the house is to buy a replacement.

> —Jack Rosenbaum, in the *San Francisco Examiner and Chronicle*

• **Rosenblatt's Law.** The duration of a modern marriage is in direct proportion to the distance from one's relatives.

> —Roger Rosenblatt, from his columns for the *Washington Post*

• **Rosoff's Rug Rat Rule.** A baby learns to say "Grandma" within an hour after she has left on the 2,000-mile trip home.

> —Denise Rosoff, APO, New York, New York

• **Ross's Law.** Bare feet magnetize sharp metal objects so they always point upward from the floor—especially in the dark.

> —Al Ross; from Jack Womeldorf

• **Rover's Law.** A dog always wants to be on the other side of the door.

> —Unknown origin; collected from a radio call-in show

• **Royko's Law.** Young people will always eat anything that is convenient, then wait until you buy some more convenient foods, and they will eat them too.

> —Mike Royko, *Like I Was Saying;* from Steve Stine

• **Rush's Observations.** (1) Expectant parents who want a boy will get a girl and vice versa; those couples who practice birth control will get twins. (2) Marriage turns lovers into relatives.

> —John Rush, Austin, Texas

• **Ruth's Law.** When you have washed all the dishes, there is always one more piece of cutlery in the bottom of the dishpan.
> —Mykia Taylor, Glenside, California

• **Ruth's Law of Mess.** Mess can be neither created nor destroyed. It is only moved around. It can, however, be turned into energy. The formula for that is $E = MC^2$, or Energy equals Mess times the speed of your children squared.
> —Ruth J. Baum, Madison, Wisconsin

S

• **Sally's Collected Conclusions.** *Child Expert's Chide:* Whatever children really like is bad for them.

> —N. Sally Hass, Sleepy Hollow, Illinois

• **Sally's Rule of Aquatic Relativity.** The neatest thing that can happen to a girl at the pool is to have two guys take her hands and feet and throw her into the water, unless the two guys are her brothers, in which case it is the worst thing that can happen to a girl.

> —Sally, a teenager known to Michael L. Lazare, Armonk, New York.

• **Samuels's Rules.** (1) Whosoever believes whatsoever is said by whomsoever is howsoever a fool. (2) Inevitability can usually be avoided by changing the outcome. (3) Most telephone call-forwarding recordings offer you a number of push-button options, the ultimate usefulness of which may be indicated by pressing "0." (4) The frequency with which you are interrupted while reading usually corresponds closely to the number of times you have asked not to be.

(5) The fastest and surest way to lose pounds is to spend an hour in a British gambling casino.
> —Arthur Samuels, Montreal, Quebec, Canada

• **Savage's Saying for Remodelers.** Always paint the back side of the house first.
> —Joy Savage, Pacific Grove, California

• **Scanlan's Law.** Wedding presents always come in pairs: two toasters, two blenders, two umbrella stands.
> —Phyllis Scanlan, Ellyn, Illinois

• **Schon's Law.** The chances of your teenager picking up the telephone extension is directly proportional to the cost per minute of the computer research database that you are, at that very time, using.
> —Alan W. Schon, Fairbanks, Alaska

• **Schulman's First Law.** Books will exceed book shelving.
> —J. Neil Schulman, *The Rainbow Cadenza;* from Neal Wilgus

• **Schwartz's Observation on Checkout Lines.** If the Law is true that the other checkout line always moves faster, this does not mean that the people in the other line are exempt from the Law. It means one of three things: (1) There is a line in the store moving even faster than theirs. (2) They are purchasing the wrong items at a faster rate than you are. Or (3) they had a lot of time to kill and now they even have more.

> —Steve Schwartz, Burnsville, Minnesota

• **Scott's Do-It-Yourself Code.** (1) Any tool left on top of a ladder will fall off and hit you in the head. (2) Any rope left dragging from any object in any location will catch on something. (3) For the successful completion of any task requiring tools, it is necessary to bleed at least once.

> —Bill Scott, Tujunga, California

• **Shaw's Solution.** If you can't get rid of the family skeleton, you may as well make it dance.

> —George Bernard Shaw; from Catherine Pfeifer

• **Shelton's Law of Bill Paying.** The bill was due before you got it.
> —John Shelton

• **Shields's Laws of New Parenthood.** *The First Outing with the New Baby Rule:* The more obvious a person's flu symptoms are, the greater the likelihood that they will insist on grabbing your baby's hands and cooing breathlessly in your baby's face. *The Rule of Unsolicited Parenting Suggestions:* The closer the relative, the more annoying the advice. *The Baby Spit-up Discovery:* The more expensive the blouse, the more copious the spit-up. *Corollary A to the Baby Spit-up Discovery:* The more times you change your blouse, the greater the likelihood that your baby will repeat the above performance. *Corollary B to the Baby Spit-up Discovery:* After your baby finishes spitting up on you, your husband will be next. *The New Parents' Amorous Desire Rule:* The more you want to make love, the greater the likelihood that the baby will wake up crying.
> —Sandra Stark Shields,
> LaCrescenta, California, cre-
> ated in January 1995 when
> her daughter was eight
> months old

• **Shopping Mall Collision Law #1.** There will be no witnesses when someone backs into your car in the mall parking lot. However, there will be one witness when you back into a car: the attorney sitting in the car you hit. *Corollary to Shopping Mall Collision Law #1.* Bigger cars back into smaller ones except when it is your fault. You will back your large car into a small expensive foreign import.

—John Culver, San Luis
Obispo, California

• **Siegel's Law of Knife Sharpening.** The first thing a freshly sharpened knife cuts is the sharpener's thumb or one of his fingers.

—Peter V. Siegel, Jr., APO,
San Francisco, California

• **Sister Cheyney's Universal Mother's Response.** All right! Share!

—From F. D. McSpiritt, Flint,
Michigan, who adds that it
applies to all situations save
those involving razor blades
or matches

• **Skinner's Law.** Anyone who owns a tele-phone is at the mercy of any damn fool who knows how to dial.

> —Jean Skinner Ostlund,
> Willmar, Minnesota, who
> learned it from her father, the
> late Arthur Z. Skinner

• **Skye's Rule.** A watched pot never boils over.

> —J. Skye, San Antonio, Texas

• **Smith's Fourth Law of Inertia.** A body at rest tends to watch television.

> —G. Guy Smith, Media,
> Pennsylvania

• **Smith's Glue Givens and Adhesive Axioms.** (1) Regardless of its intended purpose, an adhesive will always stick to your fingers best. (2) When the sophisticated two-part adhesive systems are measured accurately and mixed and timed precisely, they can be expected to work every bit as good as model-airplane cement. (3) If you break the handle on a coffee cup, consider the new space-age adhesives and then buy a new cup.

> —V. Richard Smith,
> LaGrange, Illinois

- **Smith's Laws.** *Small Appliance Axiom:* If it doesn't break immediately, it can never be fixed. *2nd Small Appliance Axiom:* If it breaks immediately, by the time it's fixed it will be too late to fix it if it breaks again. *Marketing:* You can never buy the new improved version, because a new improved version is already replacing it.
  —Jerry Smith, Florissant, Missouri

- **Smith's Rule.** When ironing a piece of clothing, the unremovable spot or unrepairable damage will be found on the last area to be ironed.
  —Suzy Smith, Tampa, Flordia

- **Smith's Suggestions to the New Graduates.** Dirty laundry never goes away.
  —Wes Smith, "Welcome to the Real World," *Modern Maturity,* June–July 1985

- **Snow's Yule Rule.** Christmas decorations of December expand to overflow available storage space in January.
  —Walter N. Snow, Overland Park, Kansas

• **Snoyer's Glove and Sock Discovery.** One size fits all means they will be either too large or too small.

> —Ernie Snoyer, Fort Worth, Texas

• **Sociogenetics, First Law of.** Celibacy is not hereditary.

> —Proposed by Guy Godin in *The Journal of Irreproducible Results* in 1975 and quickly questioned. Wrote one reader, "If your parents didn't have any children, the odds are that you won't have any."

• **Sociogenetics, Second Law of.** The law of heredity is that all undesirable traits come from the other parent.

> —"Morning Smile" column, *Toronto Globe and Mail,* February 21, 1979; from Richard Isaac, M.D., Toronto, Ontario, Canada

• **Specht's Discovery.** A condominium is just an apartment with a down payment.

> —Robert D. Specht, Santa Monica, California

• **Sprehe's Discovery.** How to locate the slow-moving traffic lane or checkout line: Get in it.

—J. Christopher Sprehe,
Shawnee Mission, Kansas

• **Stabler's Law of Moving.** If you pack up and move, when you look for something you will not find it, but when you are looking for something else you will.

—Laurence Stabler,
Gainesville, Florida

• **The Stine Dialogue for Marital Bliss.** My wife, Diane, says there are two things that are essential to a successful marriage: communication and simple politeness. I replied, "That's stupid, and I don't want to talk about it."

—Steve Stine, Skokie, Illinois

• **Stine's Laws and Rules.** *Bedtime Stories:* You cannot underestimate a child's capacity for repetition. You cannot underestimate a child's capacity for repetition.

—Steve Stine, Skokie, Illinois

• **Stockmeyer's Stock Quotations.** (1) Closet space is like money—you will use up as much as you have. (2) The more expensive the dress, the smaller the size you will be able to fit into.
> —Claire Stockmeyer,
> Washington, D.C.

• **Stoebner's Law.** Do not pour any more milk for the child than you want to wipe up.
> —Ben E. Stoebner,
> Tehachapi, California

• **Surprenant's Law of Gardening.** The easiest vegetables to raise in a garden are those you like least (and vice versa). Tastes of insects and animal pests are directly proportional to your own.
> —Donald T. Surprenant,
> Barrington, Illinois

• **Sweeney's Law.** The joy that is felt at the sight of a new-fallen snow is inversely proportional to the age of the beholder.
> —Paul Sweeney, in *The
> Quarterly,* which he writes for
> the Defense Mapping Federal
> Credit Union

• **Sybert's Law of the Workshop.** Whenever a project is undertaken, the least expensive but most important item for its completion will be forgotten (i.e., sandpaper, paintbrushes, etc.).
—Christopher Sybert,
Lutherville, Maryland

T

- **Tammeus's Rake Rule.** The last 50 leaves take as long to rake as the first 5,050.

>—Bill Tammeus, columnist for the *Kansas City Star*

- **The Teacher's Truism.** The only time parents are willing to accept their child as "average" is at the moment of birth.

>—Unknown origin; from Richard E. Fisher, Homestead, Florida

- **Teaford's Observations on Sewing Machine Personality/ Functioning.** (1) One "damn it" restores machine's functioning. (2) Two "damn its!" are self-canceling. (3) One "son of a bitch" will cause a full bobbin to immediately run out of thread. (4) Crying helps a lot.

>—Robert M. Teaford, Napa, California

• **Television Truisms.** (1) If a television character coughs, that character has an incurable disease and/or is going to die. (2) If a television character drops something, the character has the same disease Gary Cooper had in *Pride of the Yankees*.

—Kevin Whitmore,
Fairmount, Indiana

• **Thanksgiving Thought from Ann Landers.** Some of us should be thankful that we don't get what we deserve.

—Ann Landers from her column of November 25, 1993

• **Thien's Distinction.** You can always tell a home that has a five-year-old in it. You have to wash the soap before using it yourself.

—Alex Thien, in the
Milwaukee Sentinel

• **The Thomases' Observation.** No childproof bottle is absolutely "childproof."

—John and Joyce Thomas,
Grissom AFB, Indiana

• **Thorpe's Parents' Circular Rule for Rock Concerts.** It might be OK to go to a rock concert if your friend's parents will let her go, and her parents may let her go to the concert if your parents say it is OK for you to go.

> —The late James Thorpe III, Shoe String Press, North Haven, Connecticut

• **Tidler's Revision.** Don't bite the hand that has your allowance in it.

> —Lisa Tidler

• **Tiller's Theory.** Car washing precipitates precipitation.

> —George Tiller, Memphis, Tennessee; quoted in *Johns Hopkins* magazine, May 1978

• **Timothy's Principle of Crawling Infants.** Any infant who can crawl tends toward the most expensive accessible object. *Corollary 1:* Nothing is inaccessible to a crawling infant. *Corollary 2:* All babies crawl, especially when you are not looking.

> —Peter H. Dolan, M.D., Anchorage, Alaska

• **Todd's Rules.** (1) *The Bar Code Malfunction Predictability Rule.* The bar code in the check-out line, won't work on items you're embar-rassed to be buying. (2) *12 Items or Less Rule:* Cashiers may not count your items in the express lane—but the other customers will.
> —Todd Hermetz, Decatur, Alabama

• **Toner's Theory of Parenthood.** Parents never live up their children's expectations.
> —Mike Toner, Parkville, Maryland; from Christopher Sybert

• **Tropf's Discovery.** If any car you own develops a major problem, any other car you own will develop a major mechanical problem within one week.
> —David Tropf, Ph.D., Oviedo, Florida

• **Truman's Parental Instruction.** I have found that the best way to give advice to your children is to find out what they want, and then advise them to do it.
> —Harry S Truman; from Mark B. Cohen, Pennsylvania House of Representatives

• **Turk's Laws of Toys.** (1) Any child can destroy any toy within five minutes or less. (2) Any child will prefer a cardboard box to a $20 box. (3) The length of time a child plays with a toy is inversely proportional to its cost.
—Brian J. Turk, Phoenix, Arizona

• **Twain's Addendum.** Familiarity breeds contempt—and children.
—Mark Twain

U

• **Umbrella Law.** You will need three umbrellas: one to leave at the office, one to leave at home, and one to leave on the train.
—James L. Blankenship, R. C. Auletta & Co., New York

V

• **Van Dongen's Law of Heredity.** Twits beget twits.

> —Van Dongen, Saskatoon,
> Saskatchewan, Canada

• **Van Etten's Discovery.** Never argue with anyone younger than yourself; they know it all.

> —Helen Van Etten, Honolulu,
> Hawaii. It came up when her
> son was twenty-five.

• **Van Vliet's Discovery.** Why is it that when you're not expecting anything important, the mailman comes at noon? But when you're rushing to get the house payment in before they assess late charges, he comes at 8:45?

> —Jim Van Vliet in the
> *Sacramento Bee,* February 10,
> 1990; from Tom Gill

• **Vargas's Varied Laws of Jars.** A jar that cannot be opened through any combination of force, household tools, and determination will open instantly if picked up by the lid.

—Joie Vargas, Reno, Nevada

- **Vlacho's Law.** There is always one more squeeze in the toothpaste or the lemon.
                    —Unknown origin; from
                    Mykia Taylor

- **Voell's Law.** Living in the king's house does not make one the king.
                    —James W. Voell, M.D.,
                    Silver Spring, Maryland

- **Vogel's Rule.** You will never lock your keys in the car at home.
                    —W. J. Vogel, Toppenish,
                    Washington. In response to
                    the original publication of
                    this important finding, Judie
                    Wayman of Mayfield Heights,
                    Ohio, contributed this impor-
                    tant amplification: "If you do
                    lock your keys in your car
                    while you are home, your
                    house keys will be on the
                    same chain and there will be
                    no one home to let you in. If
                    you're in a real big hurry, you
                    will have left your baby
                    strapped inside the car before
                    you closed the door."

W

• **Ward's Home PC Law.** Don't buy now. In six months it will be better and cheaper. Six months later you will have to wait again for the same reason.

—Chuck Ward, Oviedo, Florida

• **Wayman's Discovery.** If driveways are far enough apart for two cars to park in front of each house on a street, there will be one car parked in the middle of each lot.

—Judie Wayman, Mayfield Heights, Illinois

• **W. C. Fields's Panaceas.** The best cure for insomnia is to get a lot of sleep.

—W. C. Fields

• **Welton's Clock-Radio Law.** Any machine tends to fix itself, if you wait long enough.

—From Michael Grant of the *San Diego Union,* who got it from a colleague on the paper.

• **Whitmore's Finding.** There are no half-empty bottles of Tabasco sauce.
> —Kevin Whitmore,
> Fairmount, Indiana

• **Wickre's Law.** On a quiet night, there will always be two good movies on TV, or none at all.
> —Unknown origin; collected
> by N. D. Butcher

• **Willey's Discoveries.** (1) The length of stay of out-of-town guests is inversely proportional to their desirability. (2) There are three absolute maxims for the handyman—your garden hose, extension cord, and ladder are always too short.
> —Boots Willey, Lehigh Acres,
> Florida

• **Wilson's Rule of Annoyance.** A caller who dials the wrong number will call a second time as soon as you have comfortably returned to your living room chair, and will act as if he or she is the one being inconvenienced.
> —Mike Wilson, Jackson,
> Michigan

• **The Winter Rule.** Winter is the season when the children leave open the doors they slammed all summer.

—Unknown origin; 1994 Ann Landers column

X-Y-Z

• **Young's Law of Conservation of Fat.**
Within any random population of adults
numbering a hundred or more, weight can be
neither gained nor lost—it can only be
redistributed.

> —David R. Young,
> McKinleyville, California

Old Saws Resharpened

We seem to be awash in inherited but wrong-headed "wisdom," flawed common sense, and bad assumptions, such as "fish is brain food," and "Rome wasn't built in a day" (who said it was?). Does "haste make waste" when putting out a fire? And some of our most treasured traditional proverbs are directly contradicted by others. Is "out of sight out of mind" correct, or do we believe that "absence makes the heart grow fonder"?

Writer and humorist Leo Rosten once reflected on the old proverb "a picture is worth a thousand words" and wrote in direct rebuttal, "OK. Draw me a picture of the Gettysburg Address." Rosten also pointed out that two heads were not better than one if both were stupid.

Fact is, many common aphorisms and bits of conventional wisdom are in need of scrapping or serious revision. Here are some proposed revisions from The Murphy Center files—created by a number of people but with several from Philip

J. Frankenfeld of Chicago, who is a master at the art of the revised proverb. It has been said that life is a do-it-yourself project without a set of instructions. Let these, then, become the instructions.

- A bird in the hand is superfluous.
- A bird in the hand usually relieves itself.
- Cast your bread on the waters and you get soggy bread.
- Don't put off until tomorrow what you can get done sometime next week.
- The early bird catches the worm, but, on the other hand, the early worm gets eaten by the bird.
- Early to bed gets the worm.
- The early worm gets the bird.
- Early to bed, early to rise, and your girl goes out with other guys. (From a guy named John, who seemed to have learned this one the hard way.)
- Exceptions disprove rules—a single exception to the law of gravity would be enough.
- Familiarity breeds.
- If at first you don't succeed, you're running about average.
- If at first you don't succeed, redefine success.
- If at first you do succeed—try to hide your astonishment.
- A fool and his money are some party.

- A fool and his money are invited everywhere.
- A fool and his money are the prime-time television target audience.
- A pool. And your money is soon parted.
- There's no fuel like an oil fuel.
- He who hesitates is bossed.
- Many hands want light work.
- Too many cooks use lard.
- I came. I saw. I refinanced.
- Never judge a book by its cover price.
- A penny saved is a penny.
- People who live in glass houses aren't very smart.
- Practice does not make perfect (golf, sex, and child rearing all prove this).
- If the shoe fits, it's ugly.
- A rolling stone angers his boss.
- A rolling stone leaves broken objects in its wake.
- As you sew, so shall you rip.
- Smiles make lousy umbrellas.
- Still waters—are polluted.
- Sweet are the uses of sour grapes.
- If wishes were horses, you could horse upon a star.
- A word to the wise is superfluous.
- All work and no play makes jack.
- Early to bed and early to rise makes a man tired in midafternoon.
- When the cat's away, it smells better.

- A watched pot is usually owned by someone without cable.
- You can fool some of the people all of the time, and all of the people some of the time, but you can't fool Mom.

Afterwords

This is the second in a series of books that will help describe elements of the real world through laws, rules, principles, and maxims.

Needless to say, the director is ever eager to collect new laws and hear from readers. Write in care of:

The Murphy Center
Box 80
Garrett Park, MD 20896-0080

Shortly after the first book, *The* [original] *Official Rules,* was published in 1978, the writer got a letter from a good woman from Pagosa Springs, Colorado, who said: "Once discovered, *The Official Rules* is like sex, indispensable."

Ever since then, the Director has relished the task of going to the mailbox for the Center's mail.

One of the benefits that accrue to those who help The Murphy Center with its research is their appointment as a Fellow of The Murphy Center. The value of such a title should be reckoned by the fact that it can be given only by the Director and cannot be bought (at least not cheaply) and cannot be taken away by anyone but the Director (who has yet to decommission a Fellow). There are now so many Fellows that it would be impossible to list all of them at the end of the book—as was the practice in earlier Center publications.

In addition, there is a select group of people who have contributed so much to the work of the Center over the last twenty years that they have achieved the rank of Senior Fellow. They cannot be thanked enough, but I will do it one more time: the late Theodore C. Achilles, Joseph E. Badger, Nancy Dickson, the late Russell Dunn Sr., Fred Dyer, M. Mack Earle, John Ehrman, Tom Gill, Joseph C. Goulden, Shel Kagan, Edward Logg, Martin Kottmeyer, Herbert H. Paper, the late Charles D. Poe, Frank S. Preston, Conrad Schneiker, Bob and Monika Skole, Marshall L. Smith, Robert D. Specht, Steve Stine, Gregg Townsend, Neal Wilgus, Bennett Willis Jr., Jack Womeldorf, Steve Woodbury, and Donald R. Woods.

Index

Acquisition. Carlisle's Rule
Address Book. Arden's (2)
Advice. Crisp's, Truman's
Aging. Breider's (2), Sweeney's, Van Etten's
Air-Conditioning. Levin's
Alcohol. Addis's (6), Clark's
Allergies. Kibble's
Allowance. Tidler's
Alternatives. Burnham's
Animals. Bryan's, Morris's
Apartments. Apartment Dweller's Law, Jaroslovsky's, Jim's, Specht's
Appliances. Smith's Laws
Art. Kozub's (3)
Assembly. Christmas Eve, Jolliffe's (2)
Automobiles. Hebert's (1), Kerber's, Norton's, Shopping Mall, Tropf's, Vogel's

Babies. Alden's (1), Hopkins's, Howe's, Kae's, New Parents', Rosoff's, Rush's (1), Shields's, Timothy's
Band-Aids. Kesulab's
Barbecue. Miller's Axioms
Bargains. Eve's, Graditor's (2)
Bath/Bathroom. Alexander's (2), Campbell's, Cripps's, Foster's, Graham's, Helen's Rule, Jackson's, Joyce's, Karen's, Kottmeyer's, Kozub's (6), Laura's, Norden's, Thien's, Vlacho's

Batteries. Christmas Morning
Beards. Addis's (12)
Bedtime Stories. Stine's Laws and Rules
Believability. Samuels's (1)
Bicycles. Jolliffe's (1)
Bills. Marsolais's (2), Shelton's
Birds. Dickson's Rules (2), Martin's
Birthdays/Birthday Parties. Burton's, Leslie's, Richman's (3)
Boiling. Ellis's, Skye's
Books. Arden's, Schulman's
Borrowing. Billings's (2)
Bugs. Davis's, Surprenant's

Car Washing. Tiller's
Cards. Buck's
Carpets. Bombeck's, Hirabayashi's, Reyna McGlone's Discovery (Corollary)
Cats. Addis's (18), Elliott's (4), Feline, Hirabayashi's, Kibble's, Little Doc's (1)
Celibacy. Sociogenetics, First Law of
Cesspools. Hauser's
Checkout Lines. Col. Tengen's, Schwartz's, Sprehe's, Todd's
Chickens. Achilles' (2)
Child proof caps. Addis's (9), The Thomases'
Children. Abby's, Achilles' (1), Addis's (3, 10), Alden's, Benchley's, Billings's (1), Burns's, Buxbaum's Rule,

Carlisle's, Crane's, Cripps's,
Forbes's, Foster's, Fred's,
Gannon's, Geist's, Gumperson's
Law of Childhood, Helen's
Rule, Hopkin's, Howe's,
Immutability (1), Kae's,
Kaplan's Law, Kesulab's,
Ladof's, Laura's, Lopez's,
Mikadet's, Morris's, Myers's,
Old Children's Law, Polsby's,
Rappo's, Rochester's, Royko's,
Ruth's Law of Mess, Sally's
Collected Conclusions, Sister
Cheyney's, Stine's Laws and
Rules, Stoebner's, The Teacher's
Truism, Thien's, Timothy's,
Truman's, Twain's, Van Etten's,
The Winter Rule
Christmas. Christmas Eve,
Christmas Morning, Jolliffe's
(2), Snow's
Cliches. Addis's (14)
Clocks. Daums's, Elliott's (3),
Linda's, Welton's
Closets. Berliner's, Stockmeyer's
(1)
Clothing. Dwyer's, Eve's,
Halperin's, Landers's, Mom's,
Olsen's, Quirk's, Smith's Rule,
Snoyer's, Stockmeyer's (2)
Clutter. Boston's, The Pirus Law,
Rist's, Ruth's Law of Mess,
Schulman's
Coat Hangers. Berliner's
Cold Hands. Carvlin's
Commuters. Lada's
Competition. Crisp's
Complaints. Hebert's (3)
Computers. Schon's, Ward's
Consistency/Constants. Quality
of Life Constant
Cookies. Kaul's (2)
Cooking. Ellis's, Johnson's,
Kozub's (5), Skye's
Cost of Living. Collins's
Credibility. Marsolais's (1)

Dandruff. Hubbard's (4)
Decisions/Decision-making.
Kaplan's Dictum
Dentists/Dentistry. Burns's (1)
Diapers. Dr. Griffitts's, Kae's
Diet. Anon's, Haviland's (2),
Samuels's (5), Young's
Dilemmas. Dorothy's
Discoveries. Alicia's, Ballweg's,
Carpenter's, DeBleyker's,
Dickson's, Haviland's, Holliday's,
Notturno's, Reyna McGlone's,
Snoyer's, Van Etten's
Dishes. Parson's (1), Riberdy's
(1), Ruth's
Disney World. Disney World
Rule, Inlander's
Distance. Jaroslovsky's, Neudel's
Divorce. Ladof's, Lipsett's
Dogs. ACW's, Addis's (16),
Bryan's, Corcoran's, Finagle's
(2), Hill's (Corollary), Rover's
Doing. Dunn's Dally
Domestic Life. Mrs. Albert's,
Broome's
Drapes. Boyle's
Drink. Addis's (6)
Driveways/Driving. Arden's,
Buxbaum's, Hall's, Harkness's,
Jewell's, Lada's, Linda's Law of
Teenage Drivers, Wayman's
Dust. Reyna McGlone's

Earthquakes. Raufa's
Eating. Anon's, Badger's,
Billings's (3), Callie's,
Churchill's, Foster's, Hubbard's
(5, 6), Momma's, Old
Children's, Olsen's, Royko's,
Whitmore's
Economics. Collins's, Jerri's
Emotion. Breider's (2)
Employment. Hood's
Encounter Groups. Gwen's
Energy. Gumperson's Law of
Childhood, Ruth's Law of Mess

Excuses. DeBleyker's
Expectations. Leslie's, Toner's

Facts of Life. Montgomery's
Familiarity. Twain's
Family. Achilles' (1), Byron's,
  Family Law, Howe's, Jump's,
  Polsby's, Rooney's, Shaw's
Fate. Hebert's (1)
Feet. Addis's (10), Ross's
Finance. Hebert's (Corollary),
  Home Buyer's
Firsts. Haviland's (5)
Football. Addis's (14)
Force. Anthony's Law of Force,
  Jake's, Jason's, Vargas's
Fuses. Bair's

Gambling. Samuels's (5)
Games. Epperson's
Garage Sales. Pope's
Garbage. Addis's (2), Bell's (4),
  Poorman's Rule, Porter's
Gardens/Gardening. Bennett's
  (2,3), Blackwell's (2), Bunn's
  (2), Dickson's Gardening
  Discovery, Gardening, Hauser's,
  Jewell's, Robert's (3),
  Surprenant's
Gifts/Gift Wrapping. Jinny's
  Sister's, Liston's, Scanlan's
Glue. Gilbert's, Kozub's (1),
  Smith's Glue Givens
Golf. Fred's
Grandchildren. Gannon's,
  Jump's, Rosoff's
Grass. Jewell's
Gravity. Lucy's
Groceries. Addis's (2)
Guests. Holliday's, Riberdy's (1),
  Willey's (1)

Hair. Dolan's, Hubbard's (4),
  Kara McVey's
Happiness. Key to Happiness,
  New Parents' (2)

Heredity. Achilles', Fischer's,
  Sociogenetics, First and Second
  Laws of, Van Dongen's
Hints. Dr. Hayes's
Hobbies. Brattman's
Home Improvement/Repairs.
  Avery's, Jane's, McClannahan's,
  Phelps's, The Poorman Flaw,
  Robert's, Savage's, Scott's,
  Sybert's
Homework. Lopez's
House/Home. Alida's, Bennett's
  (1), Home Buyer's Rule,
  Hubbard's (1, 2), McConnell's,
  Merrill's, Porter's, Voell's,
  Vogel's
Household Laws. Mrs. Albert's,
  Alexander's, Caroline's,
  Davison's, Elliott's, Finagle's,
  Hirabayashi's, Hubbard's (1, 2),
  Kozub's, Osman's,
  Preudhomme's, Rebecca's
Husbands. Alexander's (2),
  Epperson's

Ice. Kozub's (4)
Ideas. Breider's (4)
Illness. Carlisle's Nursing
  Keystone, Laura's, Myers's,
  O'Steen's, Shields's
Income. Billings's (2)
Inertia. Breider's (1), Smith's
  Fourth Law
Inevitability. Samuels's (2)
Infinity. Addis's (11)
In-laws. Mead's
Insomnia. Dickson's Rules,
  Harkness's, W. C. Fields's
Insurance. Dyer's, Riley's
Interruptions. Samuels's (4)
Investments. Rose's
Ironing. Smith's Rule

Jars. Vargas's
Jobs. Bennett's
Junk. Rist's

Junk Mail. Riberdy's (4)
Justice. Thanksgiving Thought

Keys. Key to Happiness, Mueth's,
Rooney's, Vogel's
Kitchen. Broome's
Knives. Siegel's

Laundry. Debrokowski's,
Halperin's, Holliday's, Ode,
Smith's Suggestions
Leaves. Tammeus's
Legal Advice. Ladof's
Lending. Lender's
Life. Addis's (13), Howard's,
McKinnon's, Quality of
Lightbulbs. Occam's
Lighting. Alden's (2)
Lightning. Addis's (17), Bair's
Location. Davison's
Lost and found/Lost Objects.
Abercrombie's, Alicia's, Bell's
(1), Carpenter's, Claudia's,
Debrokowski's, Hebert's (4),
Helen's Inanimate Object
Lessons, Lucy's, Rosenbaum's,
Stabler's
Lottery. Addis's (17)

Machines. Glanville's, Teaford's,
Welton's
Magazines. Addis's (8), Kozub's
(2), Pancoast's, The Pirus Law
Mail. Van Vliet's
Management. Abley's
Manners. Badger's
Maps. Addis's (4)
Marriage. Abley's, Agel's,
Blattenberger's, Carvlin's,
Cher's, Churchill's, Epperson's,
Jump's, New Laws of Marriage,
O'Neill's, Parson's (2),
Pietropinto's, Rabbe's,
Rochester's, Rosenblatt's,
Rush's (2), The Stine Dialogue
Memory. DeBleyker's

Men. Brothers's
Mess. Ruth's Law of Mess
Midlife Crisis. Nolan's
Military. Buxbaum's Rule
Milk. Ellis's (Corollary),
Stoebner's
Money. Abby's, Arden's (3),
Doudna's, Eve's, Hebert's (1),
Jerri's, Kaplan's Dictum,
Miller's Law, Moseley's,
O'Houlihan's, Phelps's (1),
Quality of Life Constant,
Tidler's
Mothers. Gwen's, Lee's, Mom's,
Momma's, Nichols's, Rappo's,
Rippetoe's, Sister Cheyney's
Movies. Wickre's
Moving. Stabler's
Music. Blay's, Burns's (3),
McKinnon's, Nolan's, Thorpe's

Nature. Addis's (11), Horton's
Neckties. Olsen's
Needs. Bell's
Neighbors. Crisp's
Newspapers. Carter's, O'Neill's
Noise. ACW's, Apartment,
Dickson's Rules, Dykema's,
Hall's
Nursing Care. Carlisle's
Keystone, Kesulab's

Objects. Abercrombie's, Bell's (2,
3), Carlisle's, Davison's, Helen's,
Karen's, Notturno's
Odds. Addis's (17), Boyle's,
Osman's
Onions. Hubbard's (5),
Johnson's, Rebecca's
Opinion. Allen's

Painting. Davis's, Savage's
Parenting. Jolliffe's (1, 2),
Parent's, Richman's, Rippetoe's,
Shields's, Sister Cheyney's,
Teacher's, Thorpe's, Toner's,

Truman's
Parties. Ear's, Neudel's
Pencils. Avery's, Napier's
Pets. ACW's, Addis's (16,18),
   Hill's, Little Doc's, Morris's
Picture Hanging. Riberdy's (4),
   Robert's (5)
Pills. Lowe's
Pins. Dwyer's
Planning. Long-Range
Plumbing. Frank's, Graham's,
   Hood's, Jane's, Phelps's (2)
Poodles. Corcoran's
Postal Service. Addis's (8)
Practice. Broome's, Van Vliet's
Pregnancy. Alden's, Bombeck's,
Pride. Dr. Griffitts's
Probability/Probabilities.
   Gumperson's Law
Problems/Problem-solving.
   Burnham's, Kaul's (1)
Projects. Ninety-Nine

Rain. Ozard's, Riberdy's (2),
   Tiller's
Reality. Haviland's (4)
Records/Recording. Blay's
Relatives. Clark's, Gannon's,
   Hubbard's (3), Husband's,
   Inlander's, Leslie's, Neudel's,
   Rosenblatt's, Rosoff's, Shields's
Relativity. Addis's (3), Sally's
   Rule
Repairs. Jane's
Rest. Alden's
Road Maps. Addis's (4)

Sales/Salesmen. Dunn's
   Observation
School. Lopez's, Myers's, The
   Teacher's Truism
Self-Help. Loch's
Sewing. Teaford's
Sex. Fischer's, Montgomery's,
   Nolan's, Shields's, Twain's
Shoes. Blackwell's, Burns's,

Landers's
Shopping/Shopping centers.
   Doudna's, Graditor's (2),
   Jackson's, Mendoza's, Shopping
   Mall Collision
Sleep. Dickson's Rules,
   Harkness's, Hebert's (2), Linda's
   Law, New Parent's (1), Rabbe's,
   W. C. Field's
Siblings. Family Law
Smoke Alarm. Callie's,
   Haviland's (1)
Snow. Norton's, Sweeney's
Snoring. Hebert's (2), Rabbe's
Soap. Thien's
Socks. Burns's, Debrokowski's,
   Irreversible, Ode, Snoyer's
Sports. Addis's, Agel's, Fred's
Status. Merrill's
Style. Landers's
Suburbs. Dickson's Rules,
   Merrill's
Success. Nichols's
Supermarket. Col. Tengen's,
   Todd's
Surface. Ballweg's
Swimming. King's, Riberdy's (2),
   Sally's Rule

Talk. Covert
Tape. Kener's, Malik's
Teenagers. Addis's (1), Anjard's,
   Burns's, Immutability (2),
   Kerber's, Linda's Law of
   Teenage Drivers, Mikadet's,
   Montgomery's, Thorpe's,
   Schon's
Teeth. Addis's (9)
Telephones. Alexander's,
   Bailey's, Campbell's, Dunn's
   Observation, Gwen's, Kae's,
   Kottmeyer's, Napier's,
   Samuels's (13), Schon's,
   Skinner's, Wilson's
Television. Addis's (5), Bailey's,
   Rice's, Smith's Fourth Law,

Television, Wickre's
Tennis. Agel's
Thanksgiving. Thanksgiving
Throwup. Laura's, Shields's
Time. Elliott's, Haviland's (3),
  O'Neill's
Toes. Irreversible Law, Kennedy
  Law
Toilet Seats. Alexander's (2),
  Burns's (2)
Toilet Training. Addis's (15)
Tools. Anthony's, Gardening,
  Hagan's, Jake's, Kaplan's Law,
  Marsolais's (1), Maslow's, N-1
  Law, Robert's (4), Vargas's,
  Scott's
Tooth Paste. Burns's (1),
  Vlacho's
Toys. Brothers's, Christmas Eve,
  Christmas Morning, Jason's,
  Jolliffe's (2), Raub's, Turk's
Traffic. Sprehe's
Travel/Transportation.
  Benchley's, Buxbaum's Law,
  Cripps's, Ear's, Geist's
Tropical Fish. Hill's
Trouble. Avery's
Twins. Billings's, Rush's (1)

Umbrellas. Umbrella Law

Underwear. Mom's
Unions. Blattenberger's
Universe. Abercrombie's

VCRs. Addis's (5)
Vacations. Cripps's
Vacuum Cleaners. Finagle's,
  Holliday's, Morgan's, Pollock's
Wallets. Arden's
Warnings. Byron's, Claudia's
Warranty/Warranties. Graditor's
Waterproofing. Horton's
Wealth. O'Houlihan's
Weather. Breider's, Horton's,
  Ozard's
Weddings. Hauser's, Scanlan's
Weekends. Fullner's
Weight. Young's
Window Cleaning.
  Preudhomme's
Winter. Norton's, Sweeney's, The
  Winter Rule
Workshops. Anthony's, Sybert's

Yellow Pages. Gustafson's

Zippers. Quirk's
Zoning/Zoning Laws.
  Lichtenberg's